Love Don't Pay the Bills

VINCENT BOZZINO

LIBERTINE PRESS

© 2022 by Vincent Bozzino

Libertine Press
34 Berkley Square
London, UK W1J 5BF

www.libertinepress.com

All rights reserved. No part of this book may be reproduced in any manner whatsoever without written permission except in the case of brief quotations embodied in social media, critical articles and reviews.

First published, 2022

Originally written in 2011, with the working title *"Hyperbole of Love"*.
First of the *"Youth Poems"* trilogy.

Printed in the United States by IngramSpark/LightingSource Inc.

Editing by Vincent Bozzino
Cover Illustration @ Henn Kim (www.hennkim.com - @henn_kim)
Author Headshot by Ilona Tuuder (www.ilonatuuder.com - @ilona_tuu)

Paperback ISBN 978-1-7392377-1-4
Ebook ISBN 978-1-7392377-2-1

A catalogue record for this title is available from the British Library.

No copyright infringement intended. Cover Illustration use is for entertainment purposes.

LOVE DON'T PAY THE BILLS

To my
scattered family

This collection has been stored at Bozzino's house,

unpublished, for 11 years.

~ I ~

My body is a temple
But how long
Can you live in the same room
And not decorate it?

~ II ~

Hot as fire
bright as the sun
it is your dense gaze
that hits me
in the deep heart.
And the sun rises to touch
the unripe apple
that is your bosom
and then,
withdraws for having dared so much.

~ III ~

So many tears
they wet me inside,
many moods
they knocked on my ribs
but I'm still waiting on this bed
your glorious body,
to petrify all impurities
of my scorn feelings
Your washing soul
quenched my arid land
and now
I am a proselyte
of every breath you take.

~ IV ~

Kiss it Better

I will be haunted by her,
beautiful poetry of human,
until I taste
the pleasure of her rhyme,
and she will no longer be
a tardive gem of my salient love.

~ V ~

Can I Be Him

Sweep me up in the wave
like blessed Venus,
your poker face
to the lover you sit next to
Yet I look at you, you melt

~ VI ~

I spend so many nights wanting you
talkative nightingale of my fantasy,
breathless bare of life,
trapped in a climbing ivy
I wait for you lopsided
sharpened in the mystery of adventure,
haunted by husk and fear,
asleep on wild chills
of a weeping willow.

~ VII ~

Now that I live September
in the loony sleeping of leaves
do not follow my ruby cloak
just to be able to get rich.
Swarming with broken-wing fairies is
the gray fabric of yours
drenched in greed
aged by this thief of time.

Now you suffer in the fog
and hide in the hills of nullity
to confess with your heart.

~ VIII ~

Tether to me
body lying in the sleep of a stem,
the only source of fragrances and graces
wherein the breath sinks its roots
and the heart of human resurfaces
Salute me
where everyone gets lost and nobody does
nobody finds himself primitive
where the goals fall
and bragging rights are born
Twist me
in the fresh wind syrup
whence I will be the dreamer and his
dream
the arrow and the witty hunter
the animal and its prey
a man and a child
but never vice without virtue.

~ IX ~

And the more I love unrequited
The more I realize
I am a flower, *indeed*
The problem is
They do not know
How to pick me

~ X ~

On my chest
a heart too moved sleeps
wherein the waters do not land
the cherry trees bloom in May
and death seems not to exist.
On my chest
a heart too shaken lies
when the sky is falling soon
and the roads part with the wind.
Babies cry at night
locked between the pillow doors
when a close smile turns off
and where there seems to be no sadness
for fatigue is never my heart's.

~ XI ~

But if suddenly one evening
we looked each other in the eye
we would make good use of it:
a simple and profound use
of us and the world.

~ XII ~

I look for your eyes but don't see them,
I look for your hands but don't feel them,
I look for your mouth and I can't taste it:
where have you flown,
wandering creature?
On another cloud to lose breath,
away in the wind to test it,
far from my hips so as not to pretend;
pusillanimous virgin,
wholesome and vagabond,
merciless daughter
of stray Valkyrie,
you stole my heart and played away,
timely reminder of female cruelty.

~ XIII ~

Disrupt the voice of the day
with the gulfs of praise that you present to me,
in the universe to the cumulonimbus
you approach with jaded eyes
throbbing, imprisoned in the sea.
Your hands like sand,
the body like silk stretched out in the sun,
mock my cry for salvation
to appear interesting to the trivial
I admire and gaze at the flirty stand
that you carry with you
the delighted dress, your rosy cheeks;
lapping with sin, you are and I
adored by your dry pity,
I speak a few words at your feet
to your curves, my soul cheers.

~ XIV ~

I lose my breath from the soot,
I wish to paint the dark
to melt your heart.
I kneel, lulled by this breeze
brushing our ankles
to bring the butterfly out,
can you stay longer?
This is my usual, flamboyant prayer
very rich regard for life,
leave your aulic torment
in my luxurious arms,
weak soul in love
and fly,
the sky is in the room.

www.ingramcontent.com/pod-product-compliance
Lightning Source LLC
Chambersburg PA
CBHW050209130526
44590CB00043B/3364